Colin Powell

It Can Be Done!

by Mike Strong

Reading Consultant:
Timothy Rasinski, Ph.D.
Professor of Reading Education
Kent State University

Content Consultant:
Dr. Lawrence A. Tomei
Lt. Colonel, USAF, Retired
Assistant Professor
Duquesne University

Capstone Curriculum Publishing

Capstone Curriculum Publishing materials are published by Capstone Press,
P.O. Box 669, 151 Good Counsel Drive, Mankato, Minnesota, 56002
http://www.capstone-curriculum.com
http://www.capstone-press.com

Library of Congress Cataloging-in-Publication Data
Strong, Mike, 1948–
      Colin Powell: it can be done!/by Mike Strong.
      p. cm.—(High five reading)
      Summary: A biography of Colin Powell, who overcame poverty and
prejudice to become a four-star general, Chairman of the Joint Chiefs of Staff,
and Secretary of State through hard work and belief in himself and others.
      Includes bibliographical references and index.
      ISBN 0-7368-9529-9 (Paperback)—ISBN 0-7368-9551-5 (Hardcover)
      1. Powell, Colin L.—Juvenile literature. 2. Statesmen—United States—
Biography—Juvenile literature. 3. Generals—United States—Biography—
Juvenile literature. 4. African American generals—Biography—Juvenile literature.
5. United States. Army—Biography—Juvenile literature. [1. Powell, Colin L.
2. Statesmen. 3. Generals. 4. African Americans—Biography.] I. Title. II. Series.
E840.8.P64 S77 2002
327.73'0092—dc21

2002000190

Created by Kent Publishing Services, Inc.
Executive Editor: Robbie Butler
Designed by Signature Design Group, Inc.

Photo Credits:
Cover, Roger Wallenburg, UPI Photo Service; page 4, Tim Page/Corbis; pages
23, 25, 33, 35, Corbis; pages 10, 13, 15, 19, 20, 38 (bottom), Bettmann/Corbis;
page 16, James A. Sugar/Corbis; page 27, Hulton/Archive-Getty Images; page
30, Allan Tannebaum, Zuma Press/NewsCom; page 36, Chris Kleponis/Zuma
Press; page 38 (top), Walley McNamee/Corbis; page 40, Getty/NewsCom; page
42, AFP/Corbis

Printed in the United States of America.

1 2 3 4 5 6 08 07 06 05 04 03

Table of Contents

— CHAPTER **1** —

Courage Under Fire

Retired General Colin Powell learned many lessons as an officer in the U.S. Army. Some of those lessons he learned on battlefields. His first battlefield lesson came in the Vietnam War (1954–1975). In Vietnam, Colin learned about fear, loneliness, and death. But he also learned about leadership.

Vietnamese soldiers wade through a river.

Facing Fear

In 1962, the U.S. Army sent Colin Powell to South Vietnam. The countries of North and South Vietnam were at war. Colin went to South Vietnam to give advice to its army. North Vietnam had a communist government. The United States did not want it to take over South Vietnam.

One day, Colin was on patrol with South Vietnamese (vee-et-nam-EEZ) soldiers. Together they walked all day through hot, sunless forest. Often they struggled through thick mud. Thick clouds of insects attacked them.

Suddenly, gunshots rang out. At the front of the line someone screamed. Colin was scared. But he moved toward the scream. He saw a wounded soldier. Another soldier lay in a stream. He was dead. The Vietcong had ambushed them.

---

communist: a person who believes that power and property should be shared by all
patrol: troops sent ahead to look for the enemy
Vietcong: a South Vietnamese communist soldier
ambush: to attack by surprise

Fear and Loneliness

After the attack, Colin felt a deep loneliness. But he had no one to tell. He didn't speak the Vietnamese language. Colin wondered why he was even in Vietnam. He hardly knew this country. Why was he ready to die for it?

The next morning, Colin woke up with the sun splashing across his face. He felt oddly joyful. For some reason, the world seemed less scary. Still today, Colin recalls that morning. That memory "got me through many a dark night," Colin says.

Protecting His Patrol

Soldiers at the front of a patrol faced special danger. Colin tried to get them to put on bullet-proof vests. The vests were heavy and hot. The soldiers didn't like them.

One day, shots again rang out. But this time, Colin heard laughter. At the front of the patrol, a Vietnamese soldier giggled.

This soldier had on a vest. The vest had a large dent in the back. The soldiers passed around a flattened bullet. The vest had saved the soldier's life. From then on, the soldiers treated Colin with greater respect.

FRENCH INDOCHINA

NORTH VIETNAM
● Hanoi

LAOS

SOUTH CHINA SEA

THAILAND

CAMBODIA

SOUTH VIETNAM
● Saigon

A Second Time

Colin returned home from Vietnam in 1963. In 1968, he went back to fight in the war. While there, he was in a helicopter crash. Colin broke his ankle, but still helped to save others. He received the Soldier's Medal for his actions.

While Colin was in Vietnam, one U.S. soldier wrote a letter that claimed he had seen some U.S. soldiers mistreating the Vietnamese people. He feared many other soldiers might be doing this, too. He said the U.S. military should not allow this.

Colin looked into the complaints. He said there might be "some cases of mistreatment" by U.S. soldiers. But he said mostly they got along well with the Vietnamese people.

Some people say Colin did not look carefully enough into the soldier's complaints. They say many of the complaints were correct. They say Colin and other leaders should have done more to make sure all U.S. soldiers followed the rules of war.

---

mistreat: to treat roughly, cruelly, or badly

What Colin Learned in Vietnam

At first, Colin had felt excited and proud to be in Vietnam. He wanted to fight communism. "It all made sense in those days," he said. But later, he felt U.S. leaders made poor decisions. He felt that was one reason the United States and South Vietnam lost the Vietnam War.

Colin saw something else in Vietnam that bothered him. Many U.S. soldiers there came from poor families and minorities. But better educated or wealthy young men sometimes did not have to go to Vietnam. Colin wanted a military that treated all people fairly. He had learned the value of fairness early, as a boy growing up in the South Bronx.

---

communism: a system in which work, power, and property are shared by all as needed
minority: a small group that differs from the rest of the population in language, religion, and so on

Chapter 2

A Poor Kid from the South Bronx

Colin Powell had little money as a child. He was not a good student. He didn't know what he wanted to be in life. His parents taught him that what mattered most was simply to do his best. What's the most important lesson you have learned in life?

Colin Powell's father, Luther

Mom and Pop

Colin was born in Harlem, New York, in 1937. Marilyn, his older sister, was five at the time. Both Colin's parents were from Jamaica. They had come to the United States to make a better life.

Colin's father, Luther, worked in the stockroom of a women's clothing maker. Later on, he was made a foreman. Luther never made much money. Colin remembers him as small, neatly dressed, and hopeful.

Colin's mother, Maud, had been a typist in Jamaica. In the United States she worked as a seamstress. Colin said she was always busy cooking, washing, and ironing. She worried about money and the family.

Jamaica: an island in the Caribbean Sea
stockroom: a room where goods are stored
foreman: a worker who oversees the work of others
seamstress: a woman who sews

Living in the South Bronx

After a few years, Colin's family moved to the South Bronx. They lived in a rough area. Gangs fought with each other. Drugs were on the rise.

Many different ethnic groups lived in Colin's neighborhood. Colin grew up unaware of prejudice against African Americans. "Everybody was in a minority," Colin said. African Americans mixed with Irish, Poles, Italians, and Hispanics. Every few blocks, there was a Jewish bakery, a Puerto Rican grocery store, or a Chinese laundry.

---

ethnic group: a particular group of people that shares the same national origin, language, or culture
unaware: not knowing about
prejudice: an unfair opinion about a group of people
Pole: a person from Poland

An outdoor market in the South Bronx, 1946

Not a Good Student

Colin was not a very good student. He also did not star in music or sports, although he liked street games. To his parents, he seemed a bit aimless.

Colin's sister Marilyn went to college. So when Colin finished high school, he decided to go to college also. He enrolled at the City College of New York.

At college, Colin joined a military training program. Colin loved the uniform and the drills. He began to model himself on a cadet leader he admired, Ronnie Brooks.

Colin had finally found something he enjoyed and was good at. He had found the military.

---

aimless: without a clear idea of what you want to do
enroll: to sign up; join
drill: a military training exercise
cadet: a young soldier
admire: to look up to

Colin Powell found in college that
he liked the military. This gave him
something to work for. He later
said, "That's what you really have
to look for in life, something that
you like, and something that you
think you're pretty good at."

Soldiers do a training exercise.

CHAPTER 3

A Four-Star Career

Have you thought about life after high school or college? What would you like to do? Colin went into the army after college. It turned out to be a good move. He received many promotions.

The "Slide for Life"

Colin had scary moments as a soldier. One came during training. Colin had to grip a hook attached to a pulley and slide along a steel cable across a river. The cable was strung between two large trees.

The instructor pushed Colin to get him started. Colin rode down the cable toward the other side at "terrifying speed." At the last second, the instructor yelled. Colin dropped 12 feet (3.7 meters) into the water below. Even today, Colin still calls this "one of the most frightening experiences" of his life.

---

promotion: advancement to a more important job
pulley: a grooved wheel that runs over a rope or cable
cable: a thick wire or rope

Discrimination

In the 1960s, the army had strict rules against discrimination. But when he was away from the army base, Colin found plenty of it.

Late one night, Colin tried to buy a hamburger at a restaurant. He knew that the restaurant would not serve African Americans inside. So from his car, he ordered from the drive-through.

A waitress came out to his car. She asked Colin if he was a Puerto Rican. Then she asked whether he was an African student at the military school. When he said he was an American, she refused to bring his food. She told him he had to go behind the restaurant to get his food. Colin simply drove away.

Colin became determined not to let bigotry affect him. Sometimes he felt hurt, sometimes angry. Mostly, he simply said to himself, "I'll show you."

---

discrimination: unfair treatment on the basis of a person's age, race, gender, and so on
determined: having made a firm decision to do something
bigotry: a strong dislike for certain other groups of people

This storefront shows a separate entrance for African American shoppers, 1964.

Germany, Here I Come

After training, the army sent Colin to a U.S. base in Germany. He was still only a first lieutenant. Even so, the army gave him command of a company.

Colin wanted his soldiers to take pride in themselves. So Colin held contests among the soldiers. He says he learned that "American soldiers love to win."

---

command: control over a group of people in the military

Marrying Alma

When Colin returned to the United States, he met Alma Vivian Johnson. The two fell in love. They married in the summer of 1962. Soon after, Colin was promoted to captain and sent to Vietnam.

Learning to Teach

After a year in Vietnam, Colin came home. He still barely knew his wife. And he had not yet seen his 8-month-old son, Michael.

The army asked Colin to teach at the Infantry School. He had not taught before. He later said that learning to teach was the most useful lesson of his life.

---

infantry: the soldiers in the army who fight on foot

Turning Point

Colin served again in Vietnam, from 1968 to 1969. When he returned, he earned a master's degree. Not bad for a student who did not do very well in high school!

In 1972, Colin was chosen to be a White House Fellow. This was his first job in Washington, D.C. It would not be his last. Over the next 25 years, Colin would work for four U.S. presidents. He would learn a great deal about politics and government.

Some lessons Colin had learned already. After the Vietnam War, many Americans did not trust their military. They did not feel proud of them. Colin wanted to bring back that trust and pride. He also saw that political and military leaders had to work closely together. Over the years, Colin has tried to make that happen.

White House Fellow: a college graduate who is paid to serve the government for one year
politics: the work or study of government

Leadership

Some students once asked Colin what makes a good leader. "Good leaders are people that other people trust," Colin said. "You can trust good leaders to do the right thing, take care of other people, and to be selfless. And to be very loyal."

How to Succeed at War

Colin did well in government work. But he liked the army better. He went to Korea as a battalion commander. He worked well with the soldiers there.

In 1974, Colin again became a teacher. This time he taught at the National War College (NWC). He says he learned an important lesson there. The government, the public, and the military all have to agree on a war for it to succeed. This did not happen during the Vietnam War, he says.

---

selfless: unselfish; noble
battalion: a large group of soldiers

Playtime

Colin always worked hard. In his spare time, he liked to work on old Volvo cars. He found it relaxing to mess around with cars. Fatherhood also kept Colin very busy. He now had a son and two daughters.

Serving the State

After the NWC, Colin commanded a division. He was now Brigadier General Powell. But Colin had proved he worked well in government, too. For the next 18 years, Colin went back and forth between the army and the government.

Colin Powell as a four-star general

A Job Review

In May 1982, Colin's new commander wrote in Colin's job review, "Do not promote." This general thought that Colin spoke out too often. Luckily, another general added a positive note to this review. Colin went on to be promoted many times.

More Hard Work

Colin became a major general. He again worked in Washington, where he gave military advice to the government. But he had a soldier's heart. He left the White House again in 1986.

For five months, Colin commanded 75,000 soldiers in Germany. He demanded hard work from his officers. But he also said, "Have fun, don't run at a breakneck speed. Take leave when you need it. Spend time with your families."

---

breakneck: rapid; very fast
leave: time spent away from the army

Back to the White House

Colin's next call from the White House came from President Ronald Reagan. He wanted Colin to work with the National Security Council (NSC). Colin agreed.

During this period, Colin helped with peace talks between the United States and the Soviet Union. The two nations agreed to cut the number of nuclear arms. They signed a very important agreement to cut arms in 1987.

Colin left the White House in 1989 to take charge of all troops on U.S. soil. This was more than 1 million soldiers.

Colin Powell with President Ronald Reagan

---

arms: weapons

Youngest Ever JCS Chairman

Later that year Colin made history. President George H. Bush asked him to be the chairman of the Joint Chiefs of Staff (JCS). This person is the top military adviser to the president and to the Secretary of Defense. Colin was the first African American named to that post. He was also the youngest chairman ever.

Crises

Almost right away, Colin had to handle a crisis. The president of Panama, Manuel Noriega (noh-ree-AY-gah), was accused of a number of crimes. Colin sent U.S. troops to Panama to arrest him and remove his government. Noriega fled but later was caught. Few U.S. soldiers were killed or injured. So overall, the mission went well.

But greater challenges lay ahead for Colin. Soon the country of Iraq would attack the country of Kuwait. The fight called *Desert Storm* was about to begin.

*Colin Powell was the first African American
to become chairman of the Joint Chiefs of Staff.*

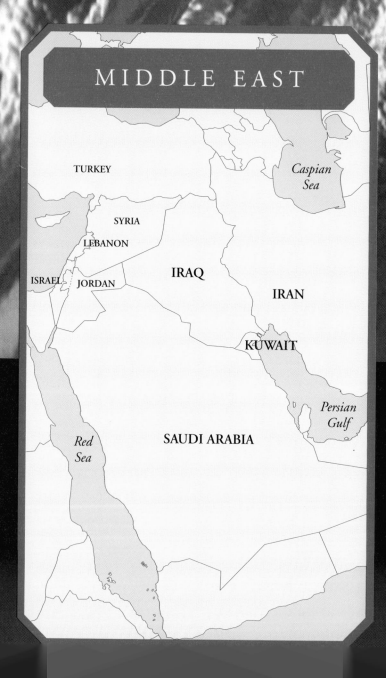

MIDDLE EAST

TURKEY

Caspian Sea

SYRIA

LEBANON

ISRAEL

JORDAN

IRAQ

IRAN

KUWAIT

Persian Gulf

Red Sea

SAUDI ARABIA

— CHAPTER **4** —

War in the Gulf

In 1990, Colin faced one of his biggest challenges. That year a war broke out between two oil-rich countries in the Persian Gulf. President George H. Bush asked Colin for his advice. What should the United States do?

All about Oil

Much of the world's oil comes from countries in an area called the Persian Gulf. Iraq and Kuwait are two of those countries.

In 1988, Iraq had been at war for eight years against Iran. Iraq had borrowed a great deal of money for this war. It needed more oil to sell to repay the money it owed.

Iraq's President Saddam Hussein planned to invade Kuwait. One reason was he wanted the oil fields that he claimed belonged to Iraq. President Hussein also thought the United States would not defend Kuwait.

Toward War

By July 1990, President Hussein's plan was clear. He had moved more than 100,000 troops close to the Kuwaiti border. Iraq was ready to attack Kuwait.

At first, Colin hoped a strong warning might change President Hussein's mind. But then 80,000 Iraqi troops crossed the border into Kuwait. This also put them close to oil fields in the country of Saudi Arabia.

U.S. troops in Saudi Arabia

"A Line in the Sand"

Colin talked to President Bush. He told the president that he should "think of laying down a line in the sand concerning Saudi Arabia." Colin worried that Iraq would attack Saudi Arabia next. He hoped a firm warning might prevent this.

The United Nations (UN) had already told Iraq to leave Kuwait. The UN placed sanctions on Iraq. These punishments made it hard for Iraq to sell oil or trade with the rest of the world. But would this be enough?

Colin wanted to avoid war, if possible. Troops would be wounded and killed in a war. He advised the president to move more U.S. troops to the area. He wanted to stop Iraq from attacking Saudi Arabia. The United States offered 100,000 soldiers to help protect Saudi land.

United Nations: an organization of nations that promise to work for world peace and security
sanction: pressure put on one country by others to make the country change its behavior

A Huge Build-Up of Troops

President Bush agreed to send more troops to the area. Two months later, there were 184,000 soldiers to defend Saudi Arabia.

Sanctions or Force?

President Hussein refused to give up Kuwait. In November, the United States sent 200,000 more troops to the area. Twenty-nine other countries also sent forces. U.S. General Norman Schwarzkopf (SHWARTS-coff) had to organize all these ground troops.

Meanwhile, the U.S. Air Force made plans for bombing attacks. Colin explained the ground- and air-attack plans to the president.

Colin wanted to send more troops and keep the sanctions. He wanted to do this rather than launch a bombing attack. But President Bush did not believe sanctions would work.

A New Plan of Attack

Colin met with Schwarzkopf to go over the plans for a ground attack. Schwarzkopf was nervous about attacking too early without enough troops. But Colin promised him all the support he needed.

The two generals put together a new plan. They explained it to the president. There would be a heavy air attack. Then ground troops would invade. They thought they would need 500,000 soldiers for the ground attack.

Powell and Schwarzkopf listen during a meeting.

---

nervous: worried, anxious

Attack from the Air

The UN gave President Hussein a deadline. Iraqi troops must leave Kuwait by January 15. The deadline passed. On January 17, air attacks started.

President Hussein ignored yet another deadline to leave Kuwait. On February 24, Allied troops attacked on the ground. The Allies soon beat the Iraqi troops. Within three days, more than 70,000 Iraqi troops gave up and left Kuwait.

The ground war lasted only a little more than 100 hours. Fewer than 400 Allied soldiers were killed. More than half of these Allies were killed by accidents or friendly fire.

Many thousands of Iraqis died. The exact number is not known. But people guess that between 80,000 to 150,000 soldiers and between 100,000 to 200,000 civilians were killed.

---

deadline: time limit; cut-off date
Allies: countries who join together for a common cause
friendly fire: shots fired from your own troops
civilian: someone who is not in the armed forces

American Heroes

After the war, many Americans saw General Schwarzkopf as the main hero. But Colin was a very important planner. He made sure that the plan could succeed. Read on to find out what he did after the war.

General Norman Schwarzkopf gives commands.

— CHAPTER **5** —

After the Gulf War

Colin has become an important leader in the United States. He tries to pass on the secrets of his success to others. He has some rules for living well. Can these help you in your life? Read on to find out.

Speaking Out

After Desert Storm, Colin went back to speak at his old school, Morris High School. The students were mostly African American and Hispanic. He reminded the students not to forget their heritage. But he also urged them to learn from other cultures.

"I remember the feeling that you can't make it, but you can," Colin said. "You can be anything that you want to be. But wanting to be isn't enough. Dreaming about it isn't enough. You've got to study for it, work for it, fight for it with all your heart and soul."

---

heritage: the history of your people
culture: the way of life of a group of people

*Colin Powell receives the Medal of Freedom
from President Bill Clinton.*

The Center of Attention

Colin became famous after the Gulf War.
He did not seek the attention. But
suddenly, people wanted to know more
about him. They wanted to hear what he
had to say.

Change of President

Bill Clinton ran against President George
H. Bush for president in 1992. Clinton
asked Colin to run for vice president.
But Colin said no.

Clinton was elected president. Colin
stayed as chairman of the Joint Chiefs of
Staff for a few months. Then he decided it
was time to go.

When he left, Colin received the Medal
of Freedom from President Clinton. The
president said, "I speak for the families
who entrusted you with their sons and
daughters....You did well by them, as
you did well by America."

---

entrust: to trust; to hand over into someone's care

The Alliance for Youth

Colin is chairman of the board for America's Promise, the Alliance for Youth. This group awards money to groups who help young people. America's Promise provides mentors for young people. It also gives them safer places to learn and to grow.

Colin Powell talks with a group of young people.

---

alliance: organizations joined together to do something
mentors: people who advise and serve as role models
for young people or for trainees in a job

A New President

George W. Bush became president in 2001. He asked Colin to be his Secretary of State. Colin accepted. He is now the president's main foreign policy adviser.

Colin helped handle the crisis when terrorists attacked the United States on Sept. 11, 2001. He is helping to organize efforts to battle terrorism.

Colin's Story

Colin rose from the streets of Harlem to high office. He did not let prejudice or bigotry hold him back. He offers young people a challenge—and hope.

Some students once interviewed Colin. He told them, "Always try to do better. I am very happy with my life, even when I've had things go very wrong. I learned from those experiences. Life has its ups and downs and you grow with those ups and downs."

---

foreign policy: a plan for dealing with other countries
terrorist: a person who uses violence and threats to scare people

Epilogue

Colin's Advice

"We need to make sure that every kid in America understands that he or she is important and that we are going to try to make every one of them a success in life."

It ain't as bad as you think.
It will look better in the morning.

Get mad, then get over it.

"Luck tends to come to people who are prepared."

Have a vision. Be demanding.

Be careful what you choose.
You may get it.

You can't make someone else's choices.
You shouldn't let someone make yours.

> "...you have to do the best
> you can with what you have. So don't
> let any negative elements in your
> background be an excuse."

Check small things.

Share credit.

Remain calm. Be kind.

It can be done!

Glossary

admire: to look up to

aimless: without a clear idea of what you want to do

alliance: organizations joined together to do something

Allies: countries who join together for a common cause

ambush: to attack by surprise

arms: weapons

battalion: a large group of soldiers

bigotry: a strong dislike for certain other groups of people

breakneck: rapid; very fast

cable: a thick wire or rope

cadet: a young soldier

civilian: someone who is not in the armed forces

command: control over a group of people in the military

communism: a system in which work, power, and property are shared by all as needed

communist: a person who believes that power and property should be shared by all

culture: the way of life of a group of people

deadline: time limit; cut-off date

determined: having made a firm decision to do something

discrimination: unfair treatment on the basis of a person's age, race, gender, and so on

drill: a military training exercise

enroll: to sign up; join

entrust: to trust; to hand over into someone's care

ethnic group: a particular group of people that shares the same national origin, language, or culture

foreign policy: a plan for dealing with other countries

foreman: a worker who oversees the work of others

friendly fire: shots fired from your own troops

heritage: the history of your people
infantry: the soldiers in the army who fight on foot
Jamaica: an island in the Caribbean Sea
leave: time spent away from the army
mentors: people who advise and serve as role models for young people or for trainees in a job
minority: a small group that differs from the rest of the population in language, religion, and so on
mistreat: to treat roughly, cruelly, or badly
nervous: worried, anxious
patrol: troops sent ahead to look for the enemy
Pole: a person from Poland
politics: the work or study of government
prejudice: an unfair opinion about a group of people
promotion: advancement to a more important job
pulley: a grooved wheel that runs over a rope or cable
sanction: pressure put on one country by others to make the country change its behavior
seamstress: a woman who sews
selfless: unselfish; noble
stockroom: a room where goods are stored
terrorist: a person who uses violence and threats to scare people
unaware: not knowing about
United Nations: an organization of nations that promise to work for world peace and security
Vietcong: a South Vietnamese communist soldier
White House Fellow: a college graduate who is paid to serve the government for one year

Bibliography

Banta, Melissa. *Colin Powell: A Complete Soldier.* Junior World Biographies. Broomall, Penn.: Chelsea Juniors, Chelsea House Publishers, 1995.

Blue, Rose and Corinne J. Naden. *Colin Powell: Straight to the Top.* Gateway Biographies. Brookfield, Conn.: The Millbrook Press, 1997.

Finlayson, Reggie. *Colin Powell: The People's Hero.* Minneapolis: Lerner Publications, 1997.

Flanagan, Alice. *Colin Powell: U.S. General and Secretary of State.* Ferguson's Career Biography Series. Chicago: Ferguson Publishing, 2001.

Passaro, John. *Colin Powell: Journey to Freedom.* Plymouth, Minn.: The Child's World, 2000.

Wheeler, Jill C. *Colin Powell.* Minneapolis: Abdo and Daughters Publishing, 2002.

Wukovits, John F. *Colin Powell.* People in the News. San Diego, Calif.: Lucent Books, 2000.

Useful Addresses

America's Promise
The Alliance for Youth
909 North Washington Street
Suite 400
Alexandria, VA 22314-1556

Internet Sites

America's Promise
http://www.americaspromise.org/

The Hall of Public Service
http://www.achievement.org/autodoc/page/
pow0int-1

PBS Online NewsHour
http://www.pbs.org/newshour/inauguration/
transition/powell.html

Scholastic
http://teacher.scholastic.com/barrier/powellchat/
transcript.htm

Index